D0518243

Getting To Know...

Nature's Children

RACCOONS

Laima Dingwall

GROLIER
B O O K S

Facts in Brief

Classification of North American raccoons

    Class: *Mammalia* (mammals)

    Order: *Carnivora* (carnivores)

    Family: *Procyonidae* (raccoon family)

    Genus: *Procyon*

    Species: *Procyon Lotor*

World distribution. North American species exclusive to North America; related species (*Procyon cancrivorous*) found in South America.

Distinctive physical characteristics. Wide band of black fur around eyes and down cheeks; ringed tail.

Habitat. Mainly brushland and forested areas, preferably near water.

Habits. Active at night; plays with food, often in water, before eating; in northern areas, sleeps much of winter but does not truly hibernate.

Diet. Buds, small animals, fish, shellfish, fruits, nuts, seeds.

Edited by: Elizabeth Grace Zuraw
Design/Photo Editor: Nancy Norton
Photo Rights: Ivy Images

Revised Edition © 1996 Grolier Enterprises, Inc.
Grolier Books is a division of Grolier Enterprises, Inc.
Original material © 1985 Grolier Limited
All rights reserved.

ISBN: 0-7172-8491-3

Have you ever wondered . . .

What do you call a bundle of fur wearing a bandit's mask?

If your answer is "raccoon," you're right. And if you could spy on a raccoon as it goes on its nightly food raids, you'd see that, in a way, it really is a bandit.

The raccoon's mask and its pointy face give it a mischievous look—and, in fact, most people know it best for the trouble it gets into. But there's much more to this animal than its mischief-making. Raccoons also are playful, intelligent, brave, and bold.

Maybe that's why few of us manage to get *too* cross with raccoons even if they:

>—eat all the corn in our garden;
>—dump our garbage can no matter how tightly we secure the lid;
>—pound on our door when they're in the neighborhood and like the smell of our supper;

Let's take a closer look at this clever and spunky animal that manages both to annoy and charm us with its many antics.

There's no mistaking the masked face of a raccoon!

Cousins Near and Far

The raccoon has two North American relatives. One is the ringtail, named for its big, bushy, black-banded tail. The other is the coati, which has such a long tail that people sometimes mistake it for a monkey.

And did you know that the raccoon even has relatives living in far-off China? The red panda, a small animal with reddish-brown fur and a bushy tail, lives in the mountains of China. And believe it or not, many scientists now believe that the giant panda, with its black and white fur and short tail, may also be a member of the raccoon family!

The red panda, also known as the lesser panda, is a member of the raccoon family. Like all raccoons, it has the distinctive face mask.

Raccoon Country

Raccoons live right across North America, except in the northern part of Canada and in the mountains of the West. They prefer to live near water, usually in brushland and among *deciduous* trees, trees that shed their leaves. But you'll also find them in open country and on farmland where there are few trees.

Raccoons have even moved into suburbs, towns, and busy cities. There they live in ravines, garages, sheds, and drain pipes. Sometimes they even make their home in attics.

The shaded area on this map shows where raccoons live in North America.

Raccoons prefer living near water and woods, but they also inhabit more populated areas. This raccoon appears to feel quite at home in someone's flower garden.

Opposite page:
To you it may look like no more than a hole in a tree—but it's home to a raccoon.

A Choice of Homes

The size of a raccoon's *territory,* the space where it lives, depends on the amount of food in the area. If there is a plentiful supply of food, the territory will be quite small. If there isn't much food available, the territory will be larger. Usually the area that a raccoon calls home covers about one square mile (2.5 square kilometers).

Within this territory, the raccoon makes a home, called a *den,* and lines it with leaves or wood chips. Sometimes a raccoon has several dens spread around its territory. You might find a raccoon den in a cave, in the hollow of a tree, or in a hollow log or stump. A raccoon may even take over an abandoned *burrow,* an underground home, that has been dug by a fox or skunk.

Raccoons don't always bother going back to their den to sleep, however. Since they are active mainly at night, they do their sleeping during the day. At the same time, raccoons have a decided taste for sunbathing. On hot summer days, a raccoon might simply drape itself over a pile of rocks or a branch and nap in the sun.

The Raccoon Up Close

If you see a raccoon from the side or the back, you might think it's a large house cat. But adult raccoons are generally bigger than cats. The average male raccoon weighs between 16 and 20 pounds (7-9 kilograms) and stands about 12 inches (30 centimeters) to the top of its back. Female raccoons are slightly smaller.

Raccoons that live in the colder, northern parts of North America are often bigger than their southern cousins. They need larger bodies because a large body stays warmer in cold weather than a small one. When northern raccoons are storing up fat in their bodies to get ready for winter, they may eat enough to double their weight. A monster-size raccoon found one autumn tipped the scales at 62 pounds (28 kilograms)—about the same weight as an eight-year-old child!

By the time winter comes, a northern raccoon's layer of body fat makes the animal look pudgy and bear-like.

Bandit Face and Ringed Tail

Of course, the first thing you notice about a raccoon is its mask. This is really a wide band of black fur that runs around the raccoon's eyes and down its cheeks.

The next feature you might notice is the raccoon's tail. It's about 8-10 inches (22-25 centimeters) long and very bushy. It has a black tip and between five and seven black rings around it. The raccoon uses its tail for balance, holding it straight out when it runs or climbs along tree branches. And when a raccoon sleeps, it wraps its tail around its body like a cozy blanket.

Fur Coats

A raccoon looks its best in the fall when its winter coat grows in. A raccoon really has two coats. One, an inner coat of brown fur, is thick, woolly, and warm. The outer coat is a layer of long black and white hairs called *guard hairs*. These help protect the raccoon from the wind. The guard hairs also are very smooth so they allow water to run off them easily. They help keep the raccoon dry as well as warm.

Opposite page: During the fall, a raccoon grows a special fur coat to keep it warm during the cold winter months to come.

17

Glow-in-the-Dark Eyes

A raccoon's sleeping habits are different from yours. It tends to sleep during the day and come out at night. For that reason, a raccoon, unlike you, has to be able to see well in the dark.

To help its night vision, a raccoon has special cells in the back of its eyes that act like mirrors. At night, the cells catch and reflect any light coming into the raccoon's eyes. This has the effect of adding to the light, and allows the raccoon to see as clearly in the dark as in daylight.

These special eyes can also produce a startling effect. If you shine a light into a raccoon's face at night, the mirror-like cells reflect the light back to you. You see the raccoon's bright eyes eerily staring back at you out of the dark.

Raccoons may see well in the dark, but they're nearsighted. Day or night, they have trouble seeing objects that are far away. They're also color-blind and see everything in shades of gray— a bit like watching black and white TV.

At night a raccoon's mirror-like eyes reflect any light shined into them. The result can be quite astonishing.

Other Senses

A raccoon has excellent hearing and a keen sense of smell. It can sniff out a mouse hidden in the grass or even an acorn buried under fallen leaves. It also has a very keen sense of touch in its nose and "fingers."

Front paw

Twinkly Toes and Nimble Fingers

The pawprints of a raccoon look something like the footprints of a human baby. But you'd never mistake a raccoon's paws for a baby's feet. The raccoon's toes are much longer, and they have short claws at the tips.

A raccoon can use its front paws much the way you use your hands. So, unlike most animals, a raccoon is able to unscrew jars, unhook garbage-can lids, and open latches. And it's smart enough to figure out how to do so, too!

Back paw

With its keen sense of smell and hearing, a raccoon can easily sniff out both food and possible danger.

On the Move

If you see a raccoon walking, you'll probably smile. A roly-poly animal, it waddles along on its short legs with its back hunched. But a raccoon can fool you. It may walk clumsily, but it can run in a burst of speed—up to 15 miles (24 kilometers) per hour—especially if it's chased by a *predator,* an animal that hunts other animals for food. But a raccoon can keep up that speed for only a short distance. To escape a predator, it usually heads up a tree.

A raccoon is a master tree climber. It walks and even runs along branches with ease. It rarely loses its footing, but if it does, it simply curls its nimble fingers and toes around the branch and hangs upside down. Then it climbs, paw over paw, until it reaches a fork in the branch where it's able to turn itself right side up.

Raccoon's pawprints

A raccoon feels as secure running along a narrow branch as you do walking on a wide sidewalk.

Coming down a tree is just as easy for a raccoon as climbing up. Unlike porcupines or cats, which always climb down a tree tail first, a raccoon can climb down head first. That's because it can turn its back feet sideways to get a good grip on the tree.

Raccoons also are fine swimmers. They often wade in shallow water looking for food, and even swim—dog-paddle style—across a pond. But they don't seem to like staying wet. As soon as a raccoon is on dry land again, it shakes itself hard to get rid of the water on its coat.

A good swimmer, the raccoon uses its bushy tail as a rudder.

Raccoon Munchies

What do raccoons eat? Practically everything, depending on what they can find.

In spring, crayfish are a favorite treat. A raccoon wades into a pool of water and pokes its long fingers into holes and under rocks. When it finds a crayfish, the raccoon plucks it out of the water and eats it on the spot. Raccoons also fish for frogs, tadpoles, and minnows, and they catch field mice, turtles, garter snakes, snails, and other small animals. Raccoons that live along the seashore catch clams and oysters.

In summer, a raccoon adds berries, nuts, and seeds to its diet. In the fall, it eats lots of acorns and insects, including grasshoppers, crickets, and beetles. Often a raccoon climbs a tree and raids the combs of honeybees. It doesn't worry about getting stung—its thick fur coat protects it!

Farmland raccoons enjoy eating corn, grapes, and apples. Sometimes a raccoon will even raid a chicken coop for the eggs.

Opposite page:
With its strong sharp claws, a raccoon can easily fish out dinner favorites such as frogs, crayfish, and tadpoles.

Water Play

When a raccoon has a meal, it doesn't always begin eating right away, as you might do. Very often, it handles the food for a time with its front paws, usually rubbing its palms forward and backwards over it. And if the raccoon is near water, it often fingers its food in the water.

Because of this habit, many people think that raccoons always wash their food before eating it. That isn't so. In some cases, when a frog or toad is on the menu, for instance, the raccoon may be getting rid of bad-tasting substances on the skin of the *prey,* or animal caught for food. But most often raccoons just seem to be satisfying their curiosity or enjoying the feel of the food in their fingers.

Raccoons also seem to enjoy rolling pebbles and stones in their hands. And sometimes when they're fishing for food, they'll pause a while just to splash about and play in the water.

Raccoons can get into a lot of mischief, but they seem to have a lot of fun at it. Will this birdbath be the scene of a midnight water fight? Or are these night raiders just dunking a snack before eating it?

Night Feeders

When darkness comes, a raccoon usually heads straight for its favorite feeding place. In the woods, that could be a spring or a pond. In the city, it might be a full garbage can. Once the raccoon has had its fill, it wanders through its territory looking for more food. If it finds some, it will visit the same spot the next night, often following the same path it used the night before.

Not all raccoons feed at night. Those that live along ocean shores feed whenever the tide is low, and that often is during the day. At that time, the water has left all kinds of tasty sea creatures lying on mud flats, in shallow pools, and along the beach. A raccoon will leave its den even in the middle of the day for such an easy and delicious feast.

Coming down from their tree perches at night, raccoons hunt for food alone or in small groups. This raccoon doesn't appear to want to share its find.

On mild winter days, raccoons sometimes come out of their dens. This one meets a beaver eye-to-eye at a local pond.

Raccoons in Winter

Raccoons that live in the southern parts of North America are active year round. There the temperature stays warm even in winter and the raccoon is able to hunt for food in nearby ponds and forests. But raccoons that live in northern areas settle down in dens—usually in the hollow of a tree—to sleep away the cold winter.

Unlike animals such as ground squirrels and skunks, raccoons do not truly *hibernate,* go into a heavy sleep for the winter. When animals go into hibernation, their body temperature drops and their breathing and heartbeat slow down. This is not so for the raccoon. It stays warm and relaxed and can easily be woken up. In fact, a raccoon often comes out of its den to bask in the sun or look for food on mild winter days. But once the weather turns cold again, the raccoon goes back into its den.

The raccoon does not store food in its den for winter munching. It eats so much in the fall that it builds up a thick layer of fat on its body and does not need much food in winter.

Mating Time

Raccoons *mate,* or come together to produce young, during the warm spells of weather between late January and early March. Raccoons in the South mate about two months earlier.

During *mating season,* the time of year when animals mate, a male raccoon wanders through its territory looking for a mate. He may travel as far as 8 miles (13 kilometers) in one night. If two males want to mate with the same female, they often fight. But the stronger raccoon doesn't always win the female. In the end, the female raccoon chooses the mate *she* prefers and turns away all others.

During mating season, a raccoon pair shares a den for about two weeks. After that, the male leaves. In northern areas the female raccoon goes back into hibernation until early spring.

About nine weeks after mating, the female gives birth. She usually has four or five babies in one *litter,* the group of animals born together. Sometimes a mother raccoon may have a litter of as many as seven babies.

Opposite page:
Two young raccoons, not yet old enough to take on the world by themselves, wait in the safety of a tree trunk for their mother's return.

Meet the Baby

A newborn raccoon, or *kit,* is about 4 inches (10 centimeters) long and weighs just 2 ounces (60 grams)—about the weight of a big cookie. The kit is covered with short gray fuzzy fur.

One of the first things you notice about a newborn kit is that it doesn't have a black face mask or rings around its tail. These markings usually grow in by the time the kit is ten days old.

The newborn kit cannot hear or see. That's because its tiny round ears are sealed and its eyes are shut. They will not open until the kit is about three weeks old. Its teeth will start appearing three or four weeks later.

The world probably looks pretty big and maybe scary when you're a new kit on a first venture out of the den.

Raccoon Mom

The female raccoon raises her family alone. Her mate plays no part in looking after the young.

As soon as her babies are born, the mother raccoon licks each one with her tongue. Then she *nurses* them, lets them drink milk from her body. When the kits are not eating, they're sleeping. They keep warm by piling on top of one another and snoozing in a big heap. If the kit on top of the pile gets cold, it wiggles around until it's snuggled into a warmer spot.

The raccoon mother stays with her kits during the day. After dark, she leaves the den to find food for herself. But she always stays within hearing distance of the kits, should they need her, and returns as quickly as she can.

A mother raccoon protects her kits from all danger. If there's a chance that an enemy has found the den, she looks for a safer spot either in another tree or on the ground. Moving the babies isn't a problem for her. With her mouth, she picks each kit up by the scruff of its neck, and carries it down the tree to the new den.

This raccoon mother has her paws full with two wriggling kits.

Growing Up

By the time a kit is two months old, it weighs about 4 pounds (2 kilograms). At this time it starts to take short trips out of the den.

Sometimes this venture into the outside world happens quite by accident. A curious kit may poke its nose a bit too far out of its den and tumble to the ground. If this happens, the kit is rarely hurt—but always surprised.

Usually, however, kits first come out when they are ready to climb down the tree by themselves. Together, the new little raccoons tag along after their mother in single file. Although a kit nurses until it is four months old, it starts to sample grass and berries on these outings. And if it's lucky enough, it might catch a tadpole, a grasshopper, or even a crayfish. With all this eating, the kit grows quickly, gaining about 2 pounds (1 kilogram) a month.

Under the watchful eye of its mother, a kit learns to leave the den and head safely down the tree.

Fun and Games

While growing up, kits spend a lot of time playing. They race up and down trees and through branches in games of tag. Sometimes they jump over one another leapfrog style. Other times they wrestle, rearing up on their hind legs and charging and grabbing one another.

If a mother raccoon thinks that playtime is getting too rough, she scolds her babies with loud growls. If that doesn't work, she might cuff them behind the ears or smack their bottoms.

Playtime is important for young raccoons. By wrestling, chasing, and pouncing on one another, kits learn how to hunt for food and to protect themselves from enemies.

As a kit gets bigger and stronger, it goes on longer outings with its mother each night. Now the young raccoon doesn't always stay close to its mother. It may trail behind her or wander ahead. Sometimes a kit goes out with a brother or sister, or it may even go out alone.

Like all youngsters, raccoon kits are inquisitive and they like to play—especially on trees. The climbing helps them strengthen their paws and develop sharp claws.

43

Such adventuring can be dangerous for a young raccoon. Predators don't often attack adult raccoons because they're such fearless fighters. But inexperienced kits make easy targets.

Young raccoons are safest with their mother nearby. She'll always rush to the rescue if one of her kits is attacked. And no raccoon fights more fiercely than a mother raccoon defending her kits.

Time To Go

By fall, the kits are about the same size as their mother. Even so, through the winter they usually stay with her in the den.

But come spring, the young raccoons leave. They're now quite ready to look after themselves. Soon they'll be starting families of their own.

A Word of Caution

Never feed or allow a wild raccoon to get close to you. Some raccoons carry *rabies,* a disease that is passed on to people through bites from infected animals. If you ever are bitten by a raccoon, tell an adult immediately.

Words To Know

Burrow   A hole dug in the ground by an animal for use as a home.

Cell   A unit of living matter. Plants and animals are made of cells.

Deciduous trees   Trees that shed their leaves at a certain time during the year.

Den   Animal home or shelter.

Guard hairs   Long coarse hairs that make up the outer layer of a raccoon's or other animal's coat.

Hibernation   Kind of heavy sleep that some animals take in the winter, during which their breathing and heart rate slow, and their body temperature drops.

Kit   Name for the young of various animals including the raccoon.

Litter   Young animals born together.

Mate   To come together to produce young.

Mating season   The time of year during which animals mate.

Nurse   To drink milk from a mother's body.

Predator   Animal that hunts other animals for food.

Prey   Animal hunted by another animal for food.

Rabies   Disease carried by raccoons and some other wild animals. It is passed on to people through a bite from an infected animal.

Territory   Area that an animal or group of animals lives in and often defends from other animals of the same kind.

Index

PHOTO CREDITS

Cover: Bill Ivy. **Interiors:** Norman R. Lightfoot, 4, 30, 33, 42. /Bill Ivy, 7, 8, 11, 12-13, 15, 19, 21, 25, 26, 29, 34, 36, 39, 44-45. /*Valan Photos:* Wayne Lankinen, 16. /*Lowry Photo,* 22. /*Network Stock Photo File:* B. Morin, 40.

Getting To Know...

Nature's Children

OWLS

Elin Kelsey

GROLIER
B O O K S

Facts in Brief

Classification of North American owls
Class: *Aves* (birds)
Order: *Stringiformes* (owls)
Family: *Strigidae* (typical owls)
          Tytonidae (barn owls)
Species: 18 species found in North America

World distribution.   Depends on species. Owls are found worldwide, except in polar regions.

Distinctive physical characteristics.   Very large eyes that point forward; ring of curved feathers surrounding each eye.

Habitat, Habits, Diet.   Vary with species.

Most common North American species.   Barred Owl, Long-eared Owl, Boreal Owl, Pygmy Owl, Burrowing Owl, Saw-whet Owl, Elf Owl, Screech Owl, Great Gray Owl, Short-eared Owl, Great Horned Owl, Snowy Owl, Hawk Owl, North American Barn Owl.

Edited by: Elizabeth Grace Zuraw
Design/Photo Editor: Nancy Norton
Photo Rights: Ivy Images

Revised Edition © 1996 Grolier Enterprises, Inc.
Grolier Books is a division of Grolier Enterprises, Inc.
Original material © 1985 Grolier Limited
All rights reserved.

ISBN: 0-7172-8492-1

Have you ever wondered . . .

Wise old owls probably appear in more cartoons, storybooks, songs, and advertisements than any other bird in the world. But they seldom have starring roles. Mostly, they perch on the sidelines looking serious and dignified and handing out good advice.

How did owls get their reputation for being so wise? Well, for one, their large eyes always seem to be studying things. And the feathery rings around their eyes remind us of the big, round eyeglasses that professors are often pictured wearing. In other words, owls *look* wise.

But the truth about real owls is that they're no wiser than any of our other feathered friends. Still, owls are amazing creatures. If you'd like to know more about these legendary birds, come fly into the pages of this book.

With its piercing eyes and no-nonsense look, this Great Horned Owl seems every bit the "wise old owl." Maybe it's just "wise" to the truth that owls, in fact, have only average bird intelligence!

Who's Who?

Owls are found everywhere on Earth, except in polar regions. From desert to forest to Arctic tundra, there is at least one type of owl for every *habitat,* or type of area where an animal lives.

But no matter where they live, owls are easy birds to identify. From the tiny Elf and Saw-whet Owls to the giant Great Gray and Snowy, owls look so much alike that even beginning bird watchers can tell when they've spotted one.

Like all birds, owls have feathers, hollow bones, and young that hatch from eggs. Yet owls are different from other birds in so many ways that they belong to their own special *order,* or group, of birds.

Most of us think of owls as rather large birds and, indeed, many are. Some, however, are no bigger than sparrows. The wee fellow shown here is a Saw-whet Owl. Tiny as it is, Elf and Pygmy Owls are even smaller.

Fluffy Feathers

From the top of their legs to the edge of their beaks, owls are covered with fluffy feathers. Some owls even have a thick layer of feathers all the way down to the tips of their toes. Owl feathers can be so soft and fluffy that if you were to close your eyes and feel them, you could easily mistake them for fur.

Most owls have dark gray and brown markings on their feathers. These colors provide good *camouflage,* they blend in well with their surroundings. An owl that is sitting still is very hard to spot. For that reason, owls—who hunt mainly at night—can rest, well hidden and undisturbed, all day long.

The fluffy-feathered Boreal Owl is named for the northern forests in which it lives. (The word boreal *means "of the north.")*

"Ears" That "Talk"

Opposite page:
Screech Owls, such as the one shown here, make a strange trembling sound up and down the musical scale. It's an eerie tune that's likely to pop the eyes of timid folks.

The little tufts that stick up on the top of some owls' heads look like ears or horns, and, in fact, they're usually called one or the other. Actually, the tufts are just special feathers and they serve a definite purpose.

When an owl is resting quietly, these feathers are only slightly raised above its head. The moment something upsets the owl, up shoot the feathery tufts.

If they stand up stiffly and a little forward, the owl is sending the same message a cat sends when it hunches its back and bushes out its tail: "I'm ready to fight for what is mine."

Standing up but leaning slightly outward, the tufts send a less aggressive signal: "You have no business here, but I'm prepared to put up with you so long as you behave."

And sometimes when an owl feels threatened and wants to avoid a fight, it'll completely flatten the tufts, as if to say, "Don't mind me, I'm just a little owl trying to get along."

Owl Eyes

Have you ever tried to catch the end of a baseball game just as the last rays of evening light were fading into darkness? Remember how difficult it was to see the ball?

That time of early night—dusk—is when most owls start their hunting. How can they find tiny gray mice when it's too dark for us to see a white baseball?

The answer is: an owl's eyes. They're enormous. If the eyes in your head took up as much room as an owl's, each of your eyes would be the size of a grapefruit! With such large eyes an owl can see much better in poor light than you can.

This Great Horned Owl and owlets, like all owls, have huge eyes that are especially equipped to catch the tiniest amounts of light. Owls, however, are color-blind, and see everything in shades of gray.

13

Most birds close their eyes by raising their lower lid.

Owls, however, lower their upper lid to close their eyes—just as you do.

But an owl can't shift its large eyes from side to side the way you can. Its eyes are fixed in their sockets just like the headlights of a car. When an owl wants to look around it has to turn its whole head.

This isn't a problem for an owl because it has a very long flexible neck underneath all those fluffy feathers. By twisting its neck, an owl can sit quite comfortably with its body pointed in one direction and its face in the other!

Many people think that owls can't see well in daylight. Actually, they see as well in daylight as you do. But they're *farsighted,* they don't see nearby objects clearly. In fact, day or night, an owl can't focus sharply on its own feet.

Like all owls, this Snowy Owl can turn its head around much further and much more comfortably than you can turn yours. But it can't *turn it full circle!*

Hidden Ears

Owls could never wear earrings. Their ears don't stick out the way yours do! Instead, an owl's ears are simply slits, sometimes very long, or small round holes on the sides of its head.

Even so, owls hear much better than you do. In fact, most owls hear so well that they can hunt just by listening for the tiny sounds a mouse or other rodent makes as it scuttles about on the ground.

Some owls have lopsided ears—one larger and higher than the other. The sound of a mouse's movements reaches each of these ears at a slightly different time. From this tiny difference an owl can tell exactly where the sound is coming from.

The special rings of curved feathers that surround each of the owl's eyes are called *facial discs.* These eye rings are very important to the owl because they help it hear. That's right: *hear!* The feathers in the facial discs are attached to muscles that control the shape of the ears. Just as a dog moves its ears to hear better, an owl moves these rings of feathers to locate sounds.

Opposite page:
A Long-eared Owl clearly displays the rings of curved feathers found around all owls' eyes.

17

Swift and Silent

No matter how well an owl can see and hear, if it were as noisy as a jumbo jet when it flew, it would have a hard time catching anything!

To help muffle the sounds of flying, most owls' wings are well padded with soft, velvety feathers. And the feathers along the leading edge of the wing are fringed just like the teeth on a comb. These feathers help reduce the flapping noises that most birds make when they fly.

Try this simple experiment. Press the fingers of each hand tightly together and clap them against each other. Repeat the same thing but with the fingers of both hands spread out. Much quieter, isn't it?

Like your outstretched fingers, the fringed edge of an owl's wing allows most of the air to pass right through. With their special wings, most owls can fly almost silently.

Most owls are fairly fast flyers. This Snowy Owl, with its wingspan of about 5 feet (1.5 meters), can work up to tremendous speeds, but it needs a long take-off and landing run.

Talented Toes

Apart from wiggling them, most of us do very little with our toes. Owls, however, have many uses for their toes—perching, walking, grabbing, carrying.

All four of an owl's strong toes have hooked claws called *talons*. Just as you stretch your fingers out to catch a ball, owls spread out their talons to make a successful strike.

Owls do this better than most birds because of their movable outer toe. In fact, if an owl wants to, it can turn the outer toe around to the back so that it makes a pair with the back toe.

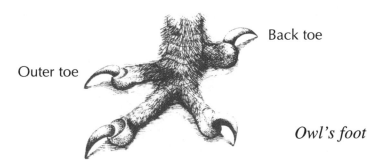

Back toe

Outer toe

Owl's foot

This young Barred Owl is in no danger of tumbling from its perch even if it falls asleep! Using two toes in front and two in back, the owl gets a solid grip on its resting place.

Mice on the Menu

Would you enjoy eating in a restaurant that served insects and mouse meat? You would if you were an owl! To an owl, such a menu would be positively scrumptious.

Owls are *carnivores*—meat is the only food that they eat. Owls never eat plants or seeds. The type of meat that an owl eats depends on how big the owl is and where it is hunting. A large owl that hunts in a meadow may eat lots of mice and rabbits, and even an occasional skunk. A small owl that hunts in a forest or desert may eat mice but it will probably eat plenty of grasshoppers, moths, and other insects as well.

Only insects, worms, and the smallest rodents have to worry about becoming a Pygmy Owl's dinner. The tiny Pygmy can weigh as little as 2 ounces (50 grams) and be no more than about 5 inches (13 centimeters) long.

Lone Hunters

Many birds feed in large groups called *flocks*. But owls need to hunt alone if they're to find enough food.

Take a minute to think about how you and your friends could collect the most eggs in an Easter egg hunt. The eggs are usually hidden in many different places. You would certainly find more of them if you and your friends spread out rather than stayed grouped closely together.

Small rodents—the objects of an owl's food hunt—live all over the meadow and forest floor. By spreading out and hunting alone, owls have a better chance of finding dinner.

Rodents Beware! The piercing eyes of a Hawk Owl are on the watch for a likely lunch.

An owl sits very still while it is hunting. Perched high atop a tree, fence post, or pile of rocks, the owl waits—carefully watching and listening for rodents. Sometimes an owl hunts by flying at a low height and watching the land below.

As soon as an owl spots its meal, it swoops silently and pounces. The force of the pounce causes the owl's legs to bend and its talons to close around its *prey*. Prey is an animal hunted by another animal for food.

A very hungry owl may have dinner right on the spot, but most carry their meal back to the safety of their perch. Mother owls carry their catch back to their babies in the nest.

As if hanging in mid-air, a Short-eared Owl seems to have spotted something interesting below. Perhaps an unsuspecting little field mouse?

A Neat Eater

Instead of picking the meat from the bones as you would when eating fried chicken, owls swallow everything, including fur and bones! Owls tear large prey into pieces before eating it, but if the prey is small enough, they swallow it whole.

With owls, the job of sorting out what can and what can't be digested goes on inside their stomach. Afterwards, the leftover bits of a meal are coughed up in sausage-shaped pellets.

It may sound messy, but an owl pellet is actually very dry and neat. The tiny bits of bone and fur inside the pellet are like pieces of a jigsaw puzzle. If we were to join enough of the pieces back together, we could figure out what the owl had eaten.

A Great Gray Owl pounces on prey that couldn't escape this bird's keen eye and razor-sharp talons.

Hard Times

When it comes to hunting, the owl has many advantages. But being an owl isn't always easy.

Like an unlucky person out fishing, an owl may spend hours without catching anything. On rainy evenings in particular, many owls go hungry. The damp ground muffles the sounds that rodents make, so it's harder for owls to locate them. Hunting is so difficult in the rain that most owls just sit it out and wait for better weather.

Most of the animals that owls hunt are *herbivores,* animals that feed on plants. If a year is too cold or too dry, there will be fewer plants and, therefore, fewer rodents. At such times some owls move to a new area to find food.

There are two separate families of owls: typical owls and barn owls. The heart-shaped face and light coloring that is common to barn owls gives this one a quite distinctive look. The barn owl's name comes from the fact that these birds often nest in the dark corners of barns.

Who...Who...Who's There?

Every owl has its own section of forest or meadow that it calls home. Known as the owl's *territory,* it is the area the owl lives in and defends from intruders.

Owls use a variety of calls to warn off unwelcome visitors. Some hoot, some whistle, and many have a call that resembles a shrill laugh. If you listen carefully on a clear night you might hear owls calling to each other. The owls in an area recognize one another by sound, and they know where their neighbors' territories are. As long as they are careful to hunt only in their own backyards, the owls remain good neighbors.

This Burrowing Owl has made its nest on a golf course. It's not known whether the person who made the sign did so out of concern for the owl or the golfers!

Finding a Mate

In late January, a male owl's nightly calls get louder and more frequent. This is the owl's *mating season,* the time of year when owls come together to produce young. The male's calls announce his ownership of a territory and his interest in attracting females. Sometimes a female answers with her own song, and the two sing an owly duet.

Except for being a little larger, most female owls look just like the males. Even a male owl sometimes has trouble telling the difference, and he is so protective of his territory that he sometimes may mistakenly try to chase away the very female he has attracted. It often can take a lot of hooting before the male realizes that the new bird is a female and not an unwelcome male!

To impress their new mates, male owls often perform trick flights or dance-like movements on a branch. And just as a man may give chocolates to his sweetheart, some male owls woo their mates with gifts of tasty mice!

Unlike some owls, a male Snowy has no trouble knowing when he has attracted a female. She is easily recognizable by the dark markings on her feathers. Male Snowies are almost pure white.

Nesting Time

When it comes to nest building, owls aren't very talented. In fact, very few build nests at all. Instead, owls often lay their eggs in a hole in a tree, in a crack in a cliff, or in a slight hollow they scratch into the ground. Many owls move into an abandoned nest that some other bird built the year before. There is even a Burrowing Owl that makes its home in the underground burrows of prairie dogs.

Some owls lay their eggs when the ground is still covered with snow. This may seem like a chilly time to start a family, but it means that the babies will *hatch,* or break out of their eggs, in spring—the time of year when there are plenty of rodents to feed them.

A Great Horned Owl mother guards the nest while the father is away hunting for food. Some owl parents choose a new mate every year, but many stay together for life.

Baby Short-eared owlets await the hatching of yet another brother or sister. Each egg hatches at a different time.

Happy Hatch-Day!

A female owl may lay as few as three eggs or as many as twelve. The number depends on the type of owl she is and on the amount of food she has had available to her. A female owl that is eating well will lay more eggs than one that is not.

The mother owl lays one egg and then waits a few days before laying the next. As a result, each egg hatches at a different time. Every baby owl, or *owlet,* has its very own hatch-day!

The eggs need both time and warmth to hatch. For several weeks, the father owl hunts for two, while mother spends all her time sitting on the eggs to keep them warm. To do this more effectively, the mother owl often plucks out some of the feathers on her underbody to make bare patches. That way, her body heat goes directly from her skin to the eggs. Her feathers don't get in the way.

Hungry Babies

Owlets are born with a covering of soft white fluffy feathers called *down*. Snuggled up to its mother and wearing its fluffy down coat to keep in the heat, an owlet stays cozy even in the chilliest storms.

Owlets grow very quickly and have huge appetites. A week-old owlet can eat much more for its size than an adult would.

For that reason, the father owl is kept awfully busy finding food for his family. Fortunately, owls are expert hunters of mice and other small animals. In fact, owls are much better mousers than any cat. Even so, the father owl may end up having to hunt both night and day to keep up with the enormous appetites of his young family.

A Snowy owlet, like all owl babies, is always ready for the arrival of its next meal.

Next step: flying. But until they do, these Saw-whet owlets spend quite a bit of practice time moving around the branches near their nest.

Devoted Parents

When an owlet is three or four weeks of age, its fluffy down starts being replaced by longer, gray and brownish feathers. The owl babies now need so much food that their mother may leave them for short periods to help their father hunt. As the owlets grow, the increasing number of dark feathers helps keep the youngsters well camouflaged while their mother is away.

Owls are very protective parents. If a hungry weasel or a curious person approaches the owlets, the parents swoop down, threatening the intruder with their sharp talons. Even the tiny owlets help to scare off enemies by hissing, snapping their beaks, and puffing up their feathery coats.

Long before they're able to fly, owlets move onto nearby branches and plants. Often people find these owlets and take them home, thinking they're lost. But the owl parents know where their babies are and are taking good care of them. It's important to leave them alone.

Growing Up

Owls learn to fly the same way that you learned to walk or ride a bicycle—with lots of practice and lots of bumps!

As the owlets develop their flying skills, the parents encourage them by dangling a tasty meal at a distance. Through practice, the young owls gradually learn to hunt for themselves. By fall it's time for them to leave their parents and find territories of their own.

The first year of an owl's life is the most dangerous. With so much still to learn about the world, many of the young owls don't survive their first winter. But those that make it to celebrate their first hatch-day have a very good chance of living to celebrate many more.

By puffing out its feathers to look threatening, a young owl can scare away an intruder.

Owls and Us

Owls are awesome birds and helpful, too. They do an important job for farmers by catching insects and rodents that like to eat crops. Farmers would have a serious problem with mice, rats, and other pests if there were no owls.

Because most owls are active at night, it's harder to watch them go about their daily routine than it is to watch other birds. But people are learning more and more about owls. Bird-watching groups conduct "owl prowls," walks meant to find and study owls in the wild. And many people are interested in protecting owls, especially the *species,* or kinds, of owls that are *endangered,* threatened with dying out.

But there still are many things we don't know about the ways and habits of owls. So the next time you're out in the woods, stop, take a careful look around, and give a few hoots. You may discover yet another fascinating fact about owls.

Words To Know

Camouflage   Coloring and markings on an animal that blend in with its surroundings.

Carnivore   Animal that eats flesh.

Down   Very soft, fluffy feathers.

Endangered   Threatened with being destroyed or dying out.

Facial disc   The ring of curved feathers that surrounds each of an owl's eyes.

Farsighted   Able to see distant objects better than near ones.

Flock   A group of animals that lives and feeds together.

Habitat   The area or type of area in which an animal or plant lives naturally.

Hatch   To break out of an egg.

Herbivore   Animal that eats mainly plants.

Mating season   The time of year when animals come together to produce young.

Order   A grouping used in classifying animals and plants.

Owlet   Baby owl.

Prey   An animal hunted by another animal for food. A bird that hunts animals for food is often called a bird of prey.

Rodents   Animals such as mice, rabbits, and gophers that have teeth especially good for gnawing. Rodents are common prey of owls.

Species   Class or kind of animal that has certain traits in common.

Talon   Claw of an owl, eagle, or other bird of prey.

Territory   Area that an animal or group of animals lives in and often defends from other animals of the same kind.

Tundra   Flat land in the Arctic where no trees grow.

Index

PHOTO CREDITS
Cover: Stephen J. Krasemann, *Valan Photos.* **Interiors:** Bill Ivy, 4, 11, 35. /*Valan Photos:* Michel Julien, 7, 19, 24, 28; Wayne Lankinen, 8, 16; Stephen J. Krasemann, 15, 37; Albert Kuhnigk, 20, 38, 44; Dennis W. Schmidt, 23; Brian Milne, 27; J.A. Wilkinson, 41. /*Network Stock Photo File:* Ken Carmichael, 12, 32./ *Federation of Ontario Naturalists,* 31. /*Hot Shots:* Doug Latimer, 42.